3-CHORD SONGS
FOR ACCORDION

ARRANGED BY GARY MEISNER

ISBN 978-1-61780-472-4

HAL•LEONARD®
CORPORATION
7777 W. BLUEMOUND RD. P.O. BOX 13819 MILWAUKEE, WI 53213

In Australia Contact:
Hal Leonard Australia Pty. Ltd.
4 Lentara Court
Cheltenham, Victoria, 3192 Australia
Email: ausadmin@halleonard.com.au

Visit Hal Leonard Online at
www.halleonard.com

CONTENTS

4

AMAZING GRACE

Words by JOHN NEWTON
From *A Collection of Sacred Ballads*
Traditional American Melody
From Carrell and Clayton's *Virginia Harmony*
Arranged by EDWIN O. EXCELL

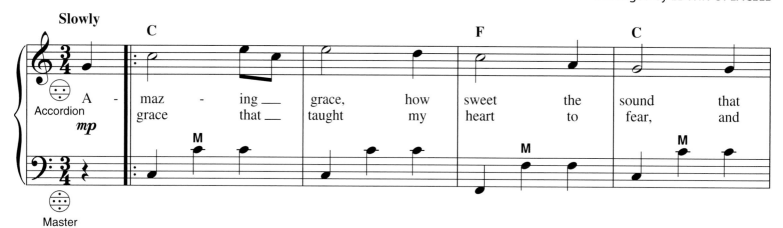

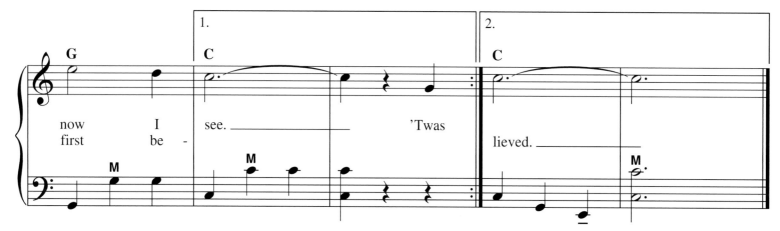

THE BIRTHDAY SONG

Traditional

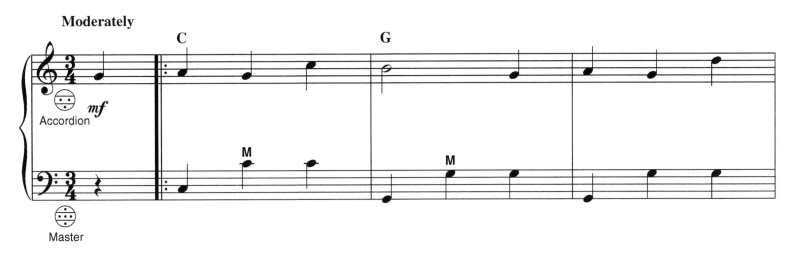

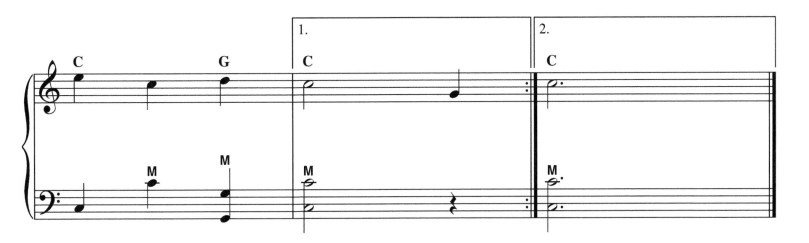

CAN CAN
from ORPHEUS IN THE UNDERWORLD

By JACQUES OFFENBACH

CARELESS LOVE

Anonymous

CHIAPANECAS

Mexican Folk Song

CIELITO LINDO
(My Pretty Darling)

By C. FERNANDEZ

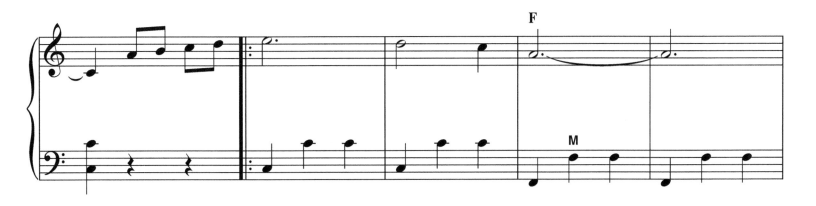

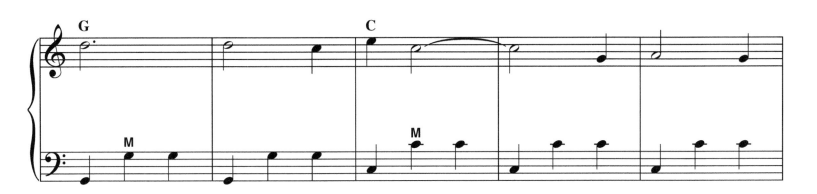

(Oh, My Darling)
CLEMENTINE

Words and Music by
PERCY MONTROSE

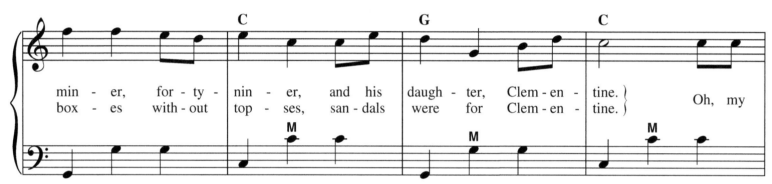

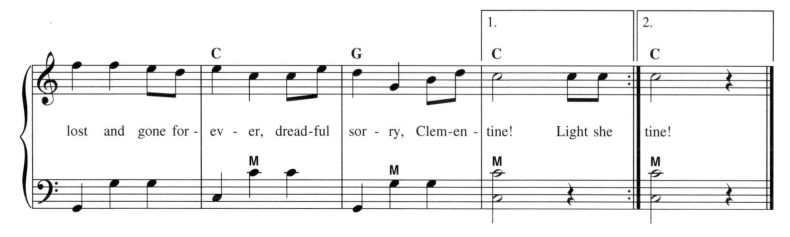

HE'S GOT THE WHOLE WORLD IN HIS HANDS

Traditional Spiritual

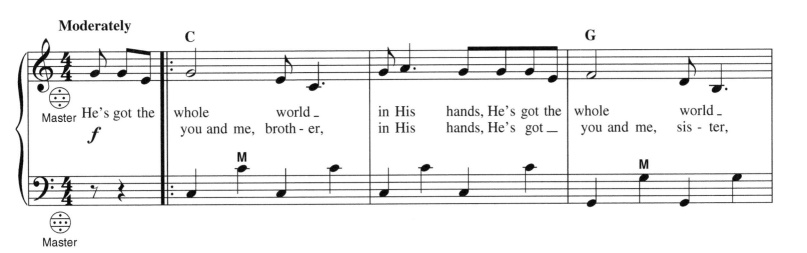

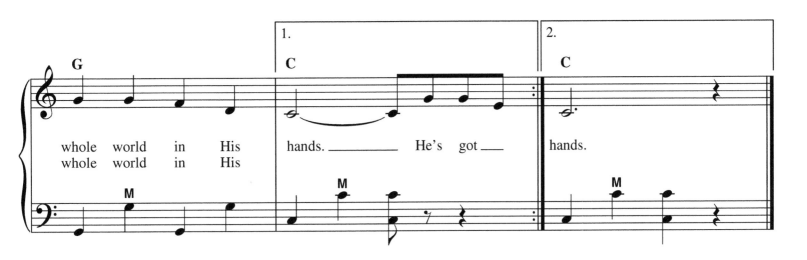

DANNY BOY

Words by FREDERICK EDWARD WEATHERLY
Traditional Irish Folk Melody

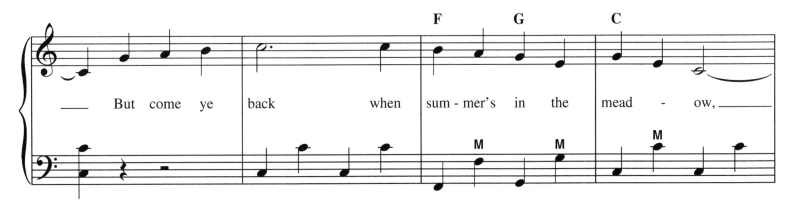

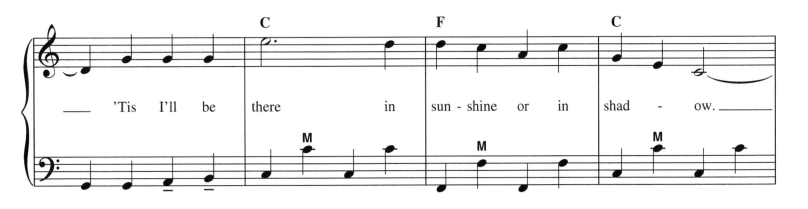

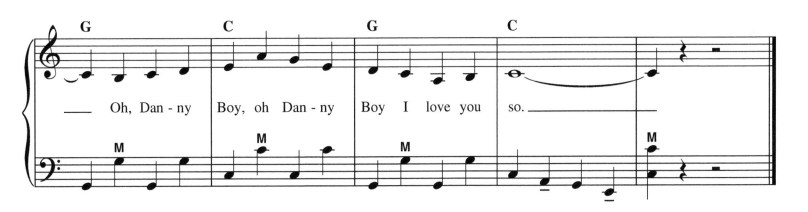

DU, DU, LIEGST MIR IM HERZEN
(You, You Weigh on My Heart)

German Folksong

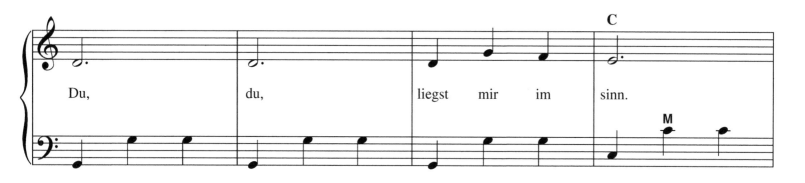

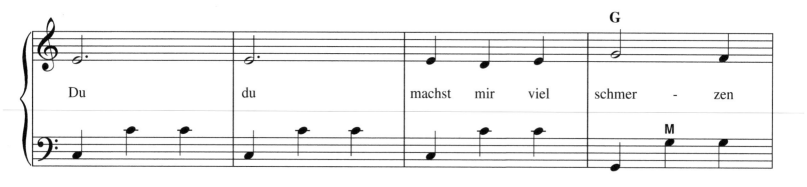

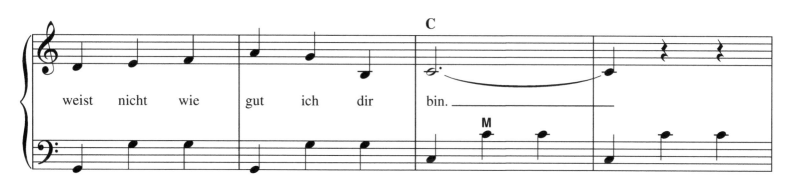

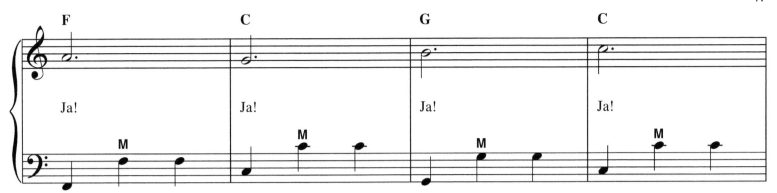

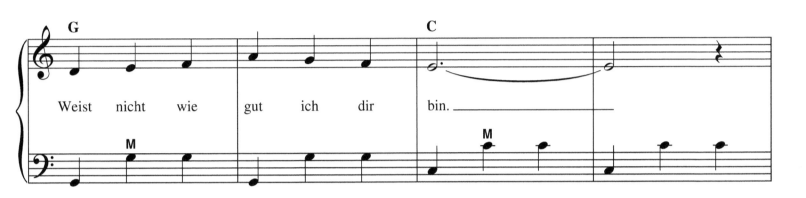

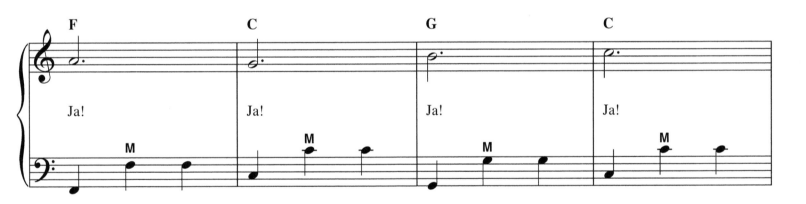

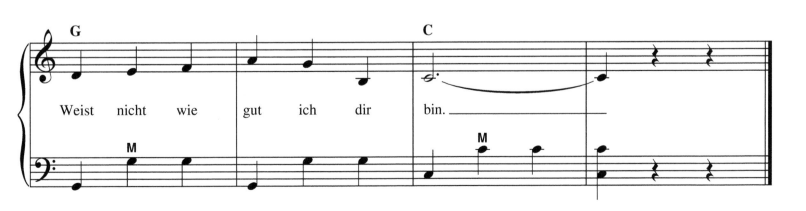

FOR HE'S A JOLLY GOOD FELLOW

Traditional

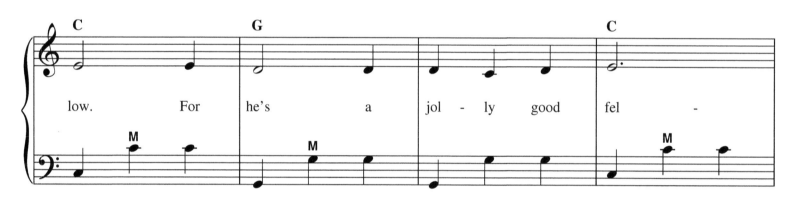

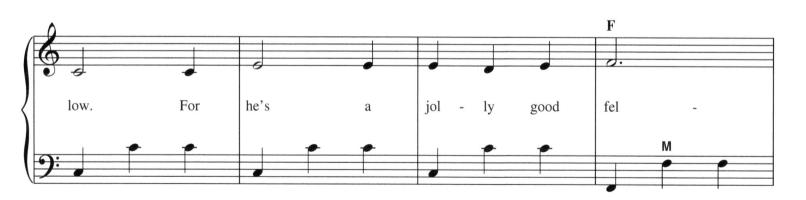

To Coda

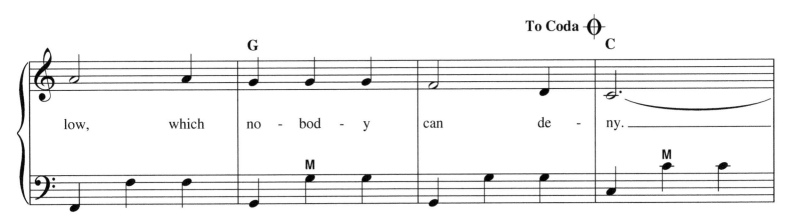

low,   which no - bod - y can de - ny. ___

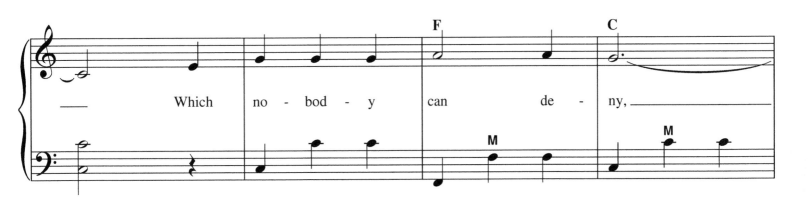

___ Which no - bod - y can de - ny, ___

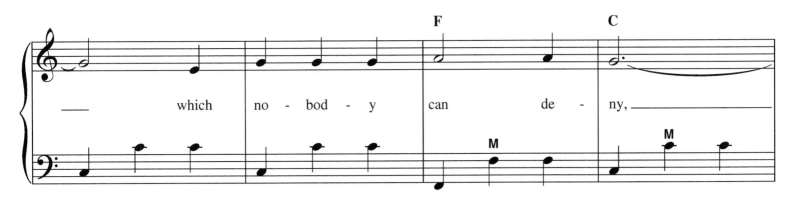

___ which no - bod - y can de - ny, ___

D.S. al Coda

___ For

CODA

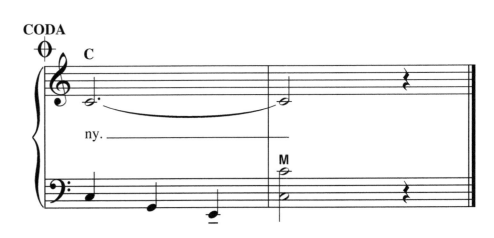

ny. ___

GET ALONG, LITTLE DOGIES

Traditional

21

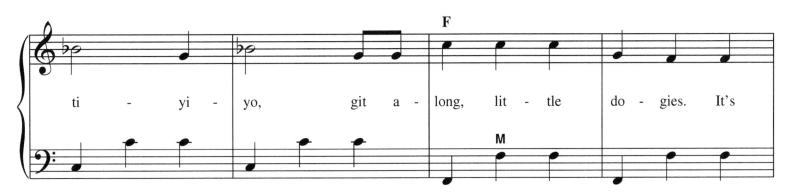

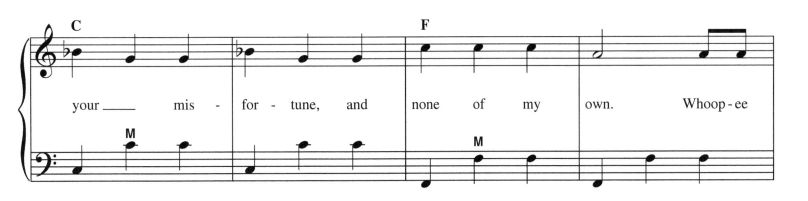

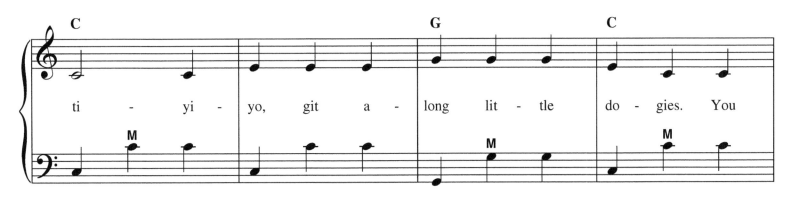

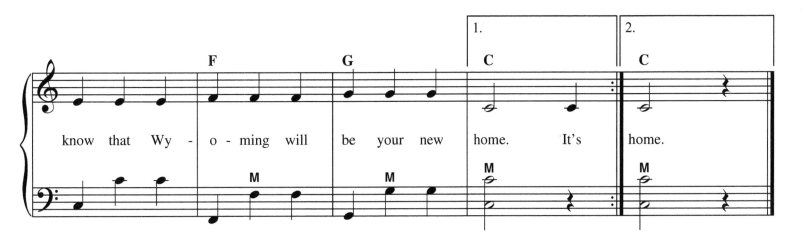

HOME SWEET HOME

Words by JOHN HOWARD PAYNE
Music by HENRY R. BISHOP

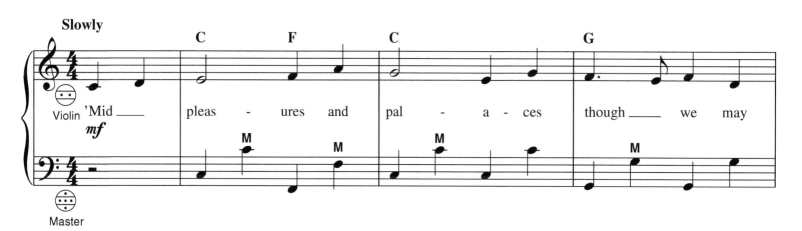

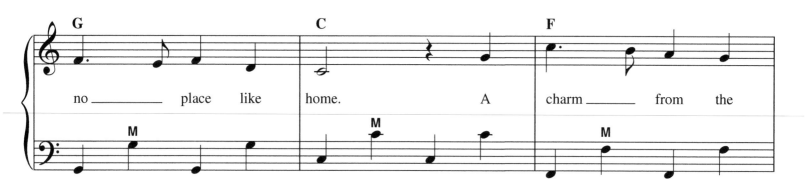

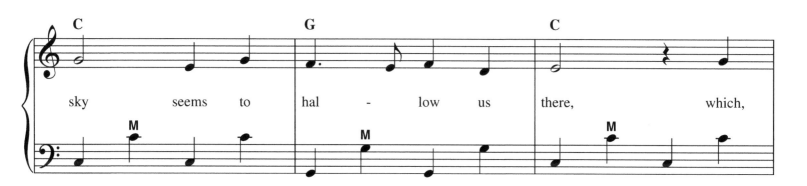

23

JUST A CLOSER WALK WITH THEE

Traditional
Arranged by KENNETH MORRIS

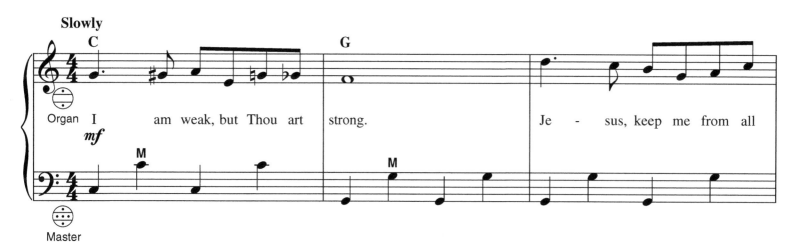

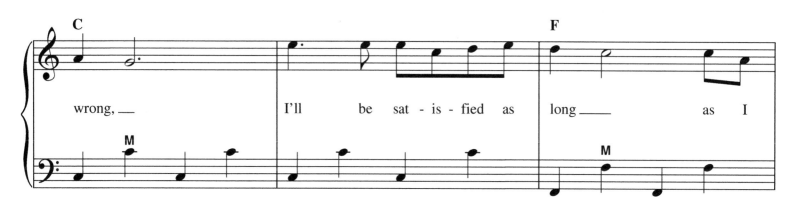

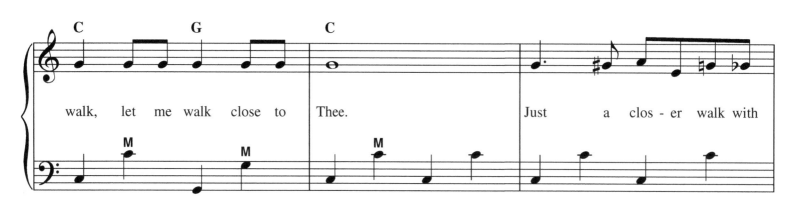

Thee,   grant   it, Je - sus, is my   plea, _____

dai - ly walk-ing close to   Thee. _____   Let it   be,   dear Lord, let it

be.   Let   it   be,   dear Lord, let it   be.

LA GOLONDRINA

By N. SERRADELL

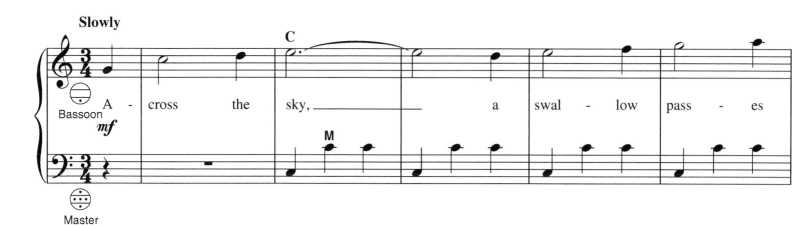

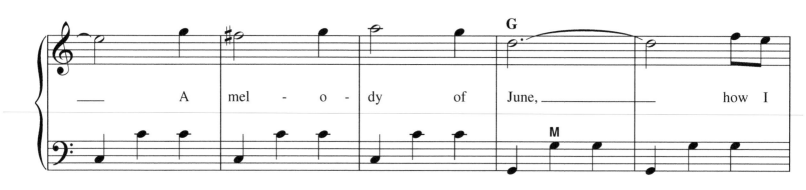

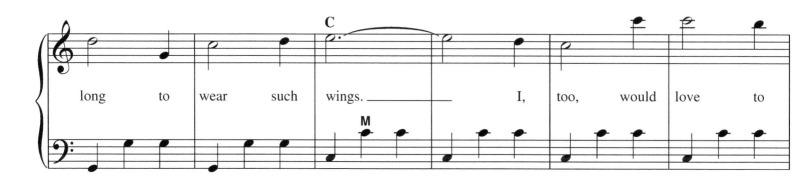

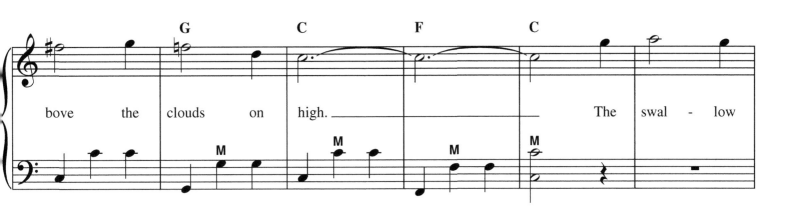

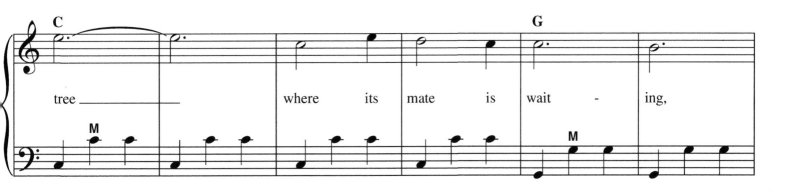

28

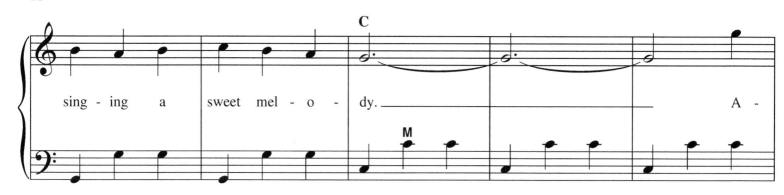

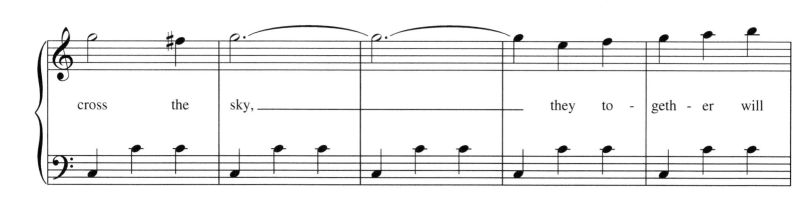

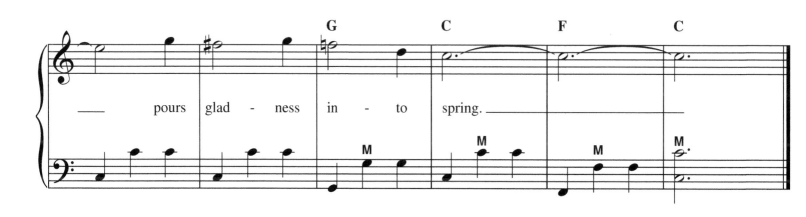

LA PALOMA BLANCA
(The White Dove)

By S. YRADIER

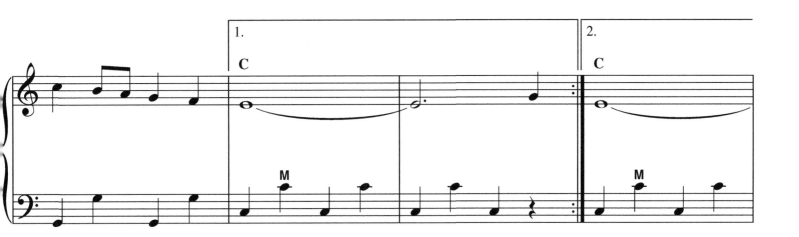

LOCH LOMOND

Scottish Folksong

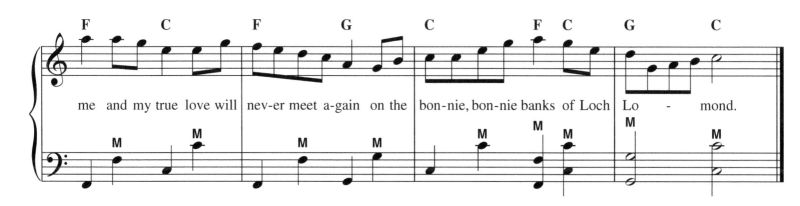

MY COUNTRY, 'TIS OF THEE
(America)

Words by SAMUEL FRANCIS SMITH
Music from *Thesaurus Musicus*

MARINE'S HYMN

Words by HENRY C. DAVIS
Melody based on a theme by JACQUES OFFENBACH

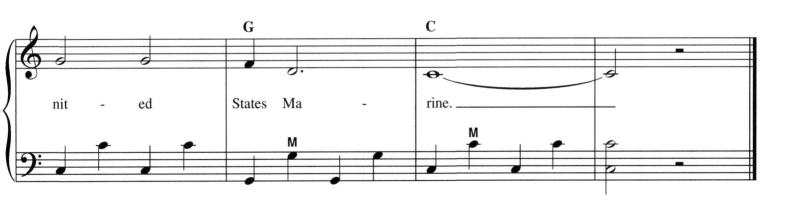

ODE TO JOY
from SYMPHONY NO. 9 IN D MINOR, FOURTH MOVEMENT CHORAL THEME

Words by HENRY VAN DYKE
Music by LUDWIG VAN BEETHOVEN

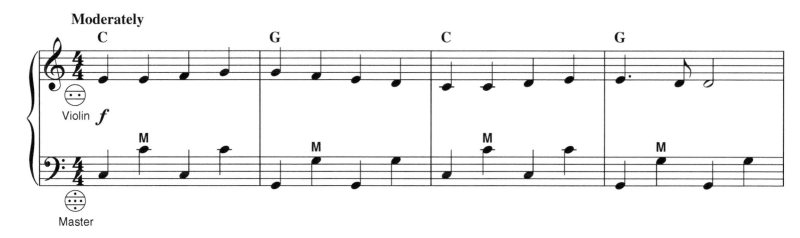

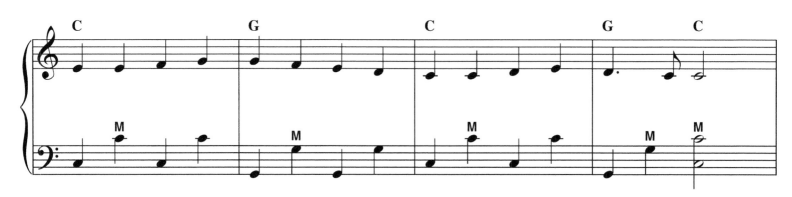

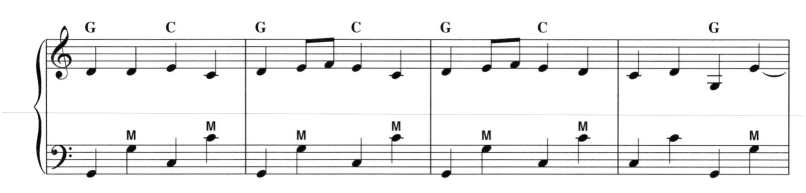

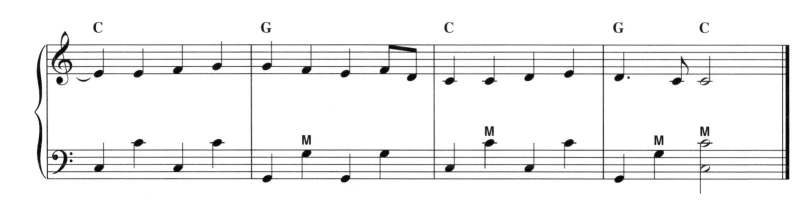

OH! SUSANNA

Words and Music by
STEPHEN C. FOSTER

ON TOP OF OLD SMOKY

Kentucky Mountain Folksong

THE WABASH CANNON BALL

Hobo Song

THERE IS A TAVERN IN THE TOWN

Traditional Drinking Song

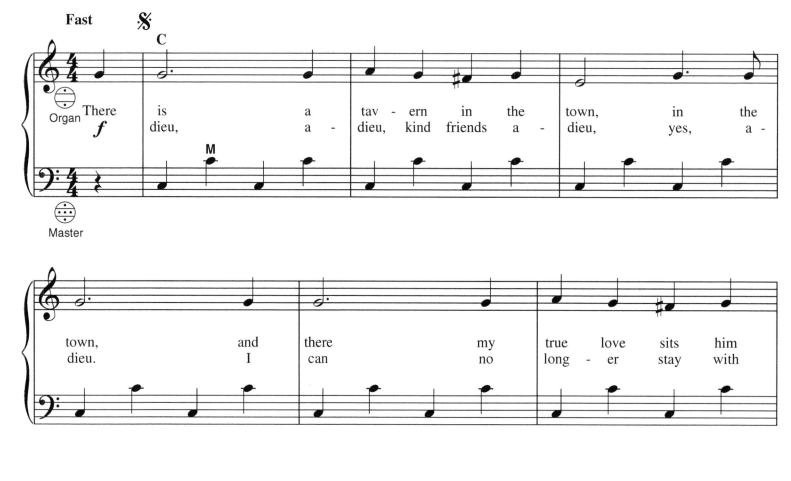

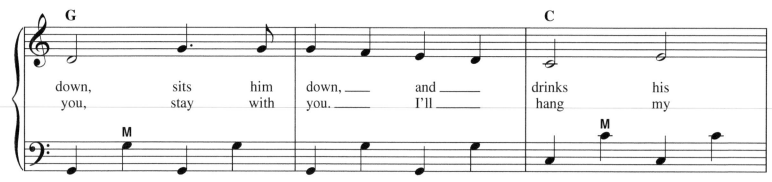

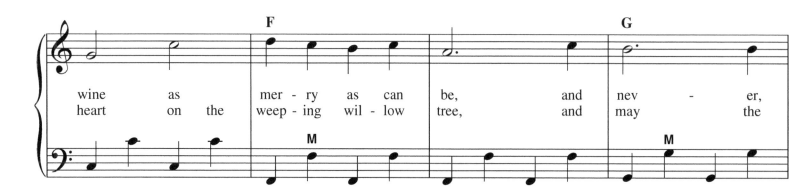

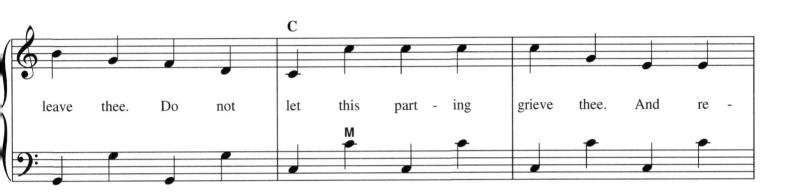

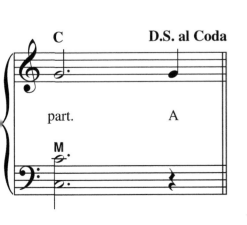

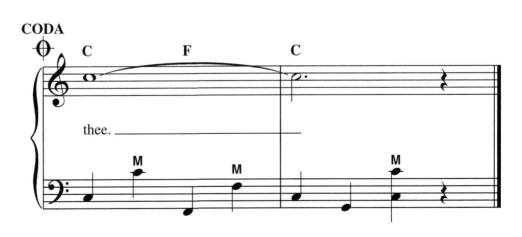

WHISPERING HOPE

Words and Music by
ALICE HAWTHORNE

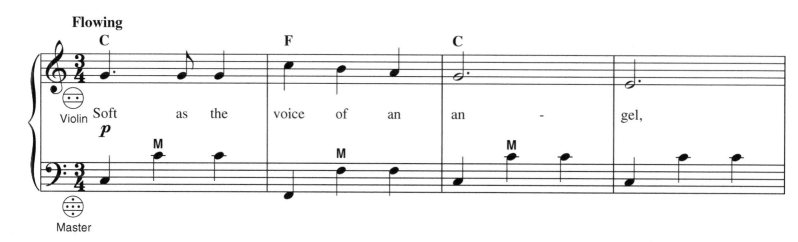

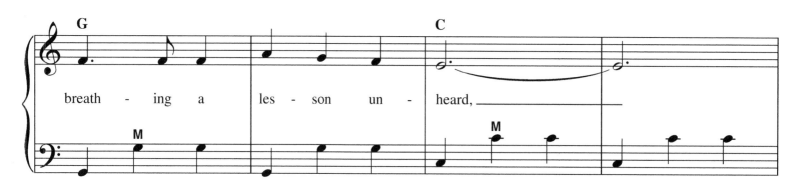

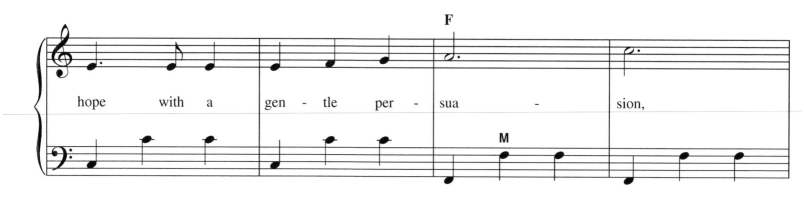

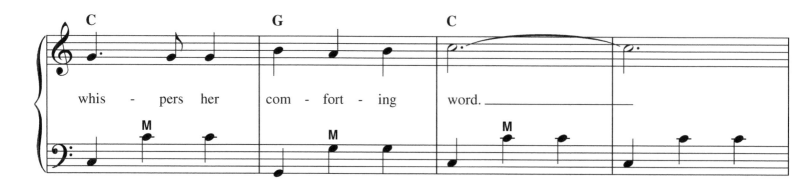

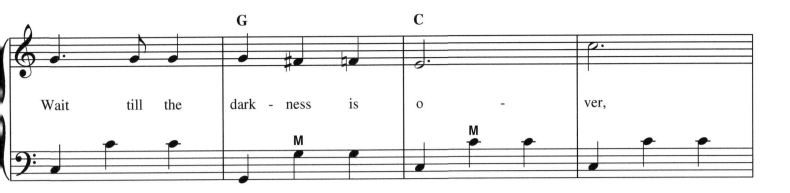

Wait till the dark - ness is o - ver,

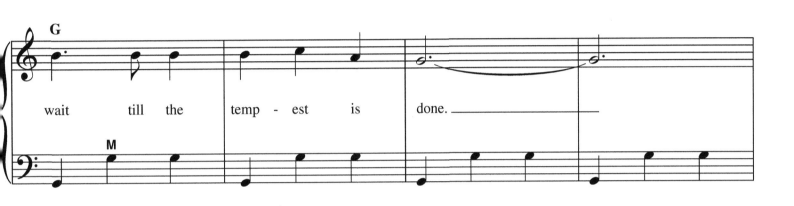

wait till the temp - est is done. ____

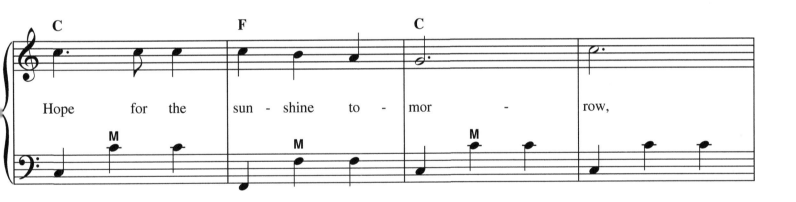

Hope for the sun - shine to - mor - row,

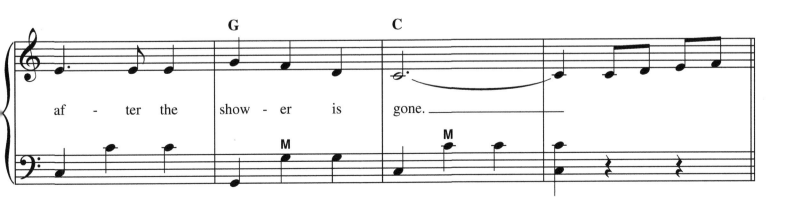

af - ter the show - er is gone. ____

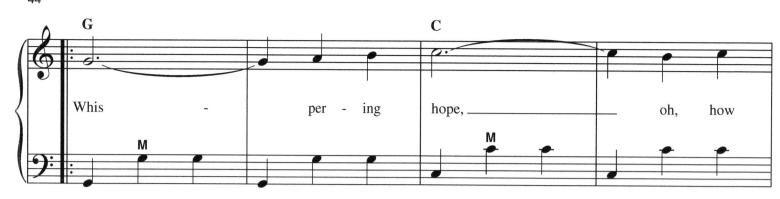

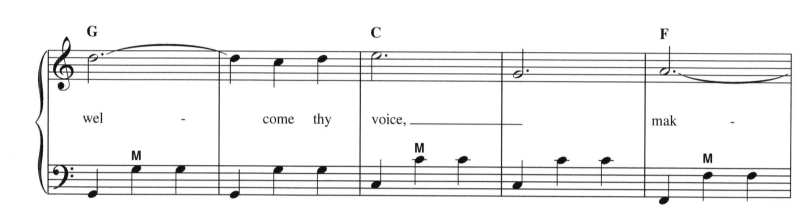

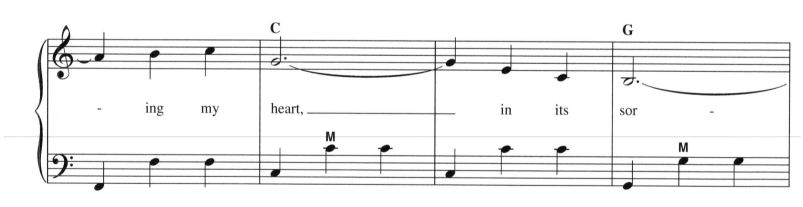

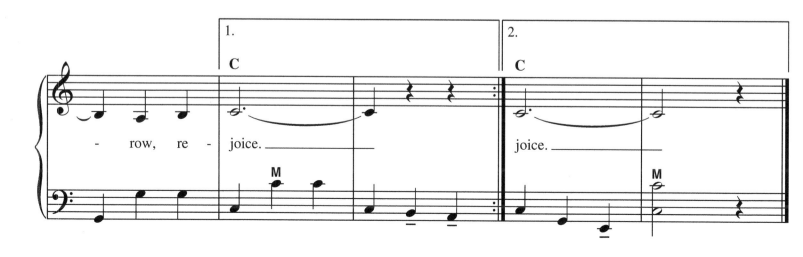

YANKEE DOODLE

Traditional

THE YELLOW ROSE OF TEXAS

Words and Music by J.K., 1858

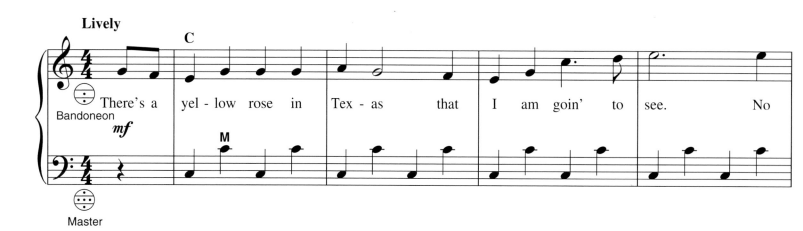

There's a yel - low rose in Tex - as that I am goin' to see. No

oth - er fel - low loves her, no - bod - y, on - ly me. She

cried so when I left her, it like to broke my heart. And

if I ev - er find her, we nev - er - more will part. She's the

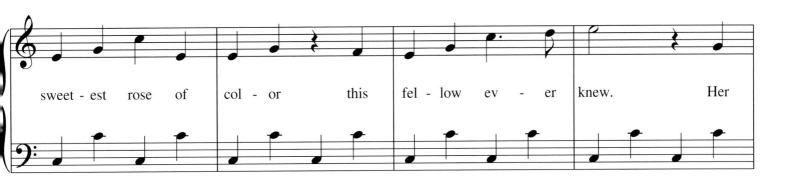

sweet - est rose of col - or this fel - low ev - er knew. Her

eyes are bright as dia - monds, they spar - kle like the dew. You may

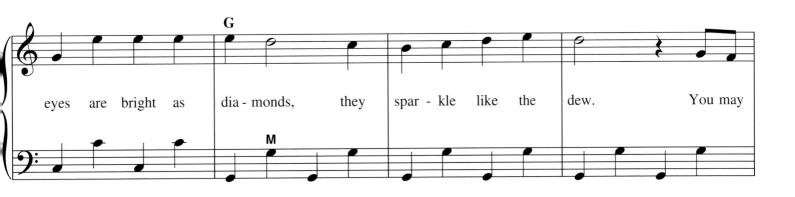

talk a - bout your dear - est May, and sing of Ro - sa Lee, but the

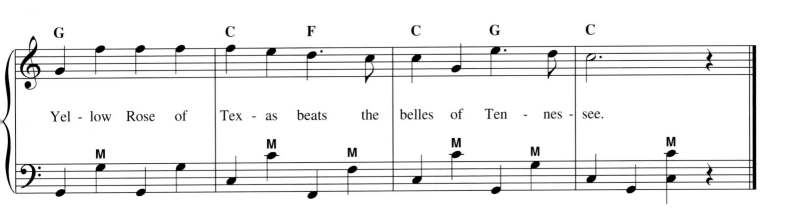

Yel - low Rose of Tex - as beats the belles of Ten - nes - see.

A COLLECTION OF ALL-TIME FAVORITES
FOR ACCORDION

ACCORDION FAVORITES
arr. Gary Meisner
16 all-time favorites, arranged for accordion, including: Can't Smile Without You • Could I Have This Dance • Endless Love • Memory • Sunrise, Sunset • I.O.U. • and more.
00359012..............................$12.99

ALL-TIME FAVORITES FOR ACCORDION
arr. Gary Meisner
20 must-know standards arranged for accordions. Includes: Ain't Misbehavin' • Autumn Leaves • Crazy • Hello, Dolly! • Hey, Good Lookin' • Moon River • Speak Softly, Love • Unchained Melody • The Way We Were • Zip-A-Dee-Doo-Dah • and more.
00311088..............................$12.99

THE BEATLES FOR ACCORDION
17 hits from the Lads from Liverpool have been arranged for accordion. Includes: All You Need Is Love • Eleanor Rigby • The Fool on the Hill • Here Comes the Sun • Hey Jude • In My Life • Let It Be • Ob-La-Di, Ob-La-Da • Penny Lane • When I'm Sixty-Four • Yesterday • and more.
00268724 ....$14.99

BROADWAY FAVORITES
arr. Ken Kotwitz
A collection of 17 wonderful show songs, including: Don't Cry for Me Argentina • Getting to Know You • If I Were a Rich Man • Oklahoma • People Will Say We're in Love • We Kiss in a Shadow.
00490157..............................$10.99

DISNEY SONGS FOR ACCORDION – 3RD EDITION
13 Disney favorites especially arranged for accordion, including: Be Our Guest • Beauty and the Beast • Can You Feel the Love Tonight • Chim Chim Cher-ee • It's a Small World • Let It Go • Under the Sea • A Whole New World • You'll Be in My Heart • Zip-A-Dee-Doo-Dah • and more!
00152508 ....$12.99

FIRST 50 SONGS YOU SHOULD PLAY ON THE ACCORDION
arr. Gary Meisner
If you're new to the accordion, you are probably eager to learn some songs. This book provides 50 simplified arrangements of must-know popular standards, folk songs and show tunes, including: All of Me • Beer Barrel Polka • Carnival of Venice • Edelweiss • Hava Nagila (Let's Be Happy) • Hernando's Hideaway • Jambalaya (On the Bayou) • Lady of Spain • Moon River • 'O Sole Mio • Sentimental Journey • Somewhere, My Love • That's Amore (That's Love) • Under Paris Skies • and more. Includes lyrics when applicable.
00250269 ....$16.99

FRENCH SONGS FOR ACCORDION
arr. Gary Meisner
A très magnifique collection of 17 French standards arranged for the accordion. Includes: Autumn Leaves • Beyond the Sea • C'est Magnifique • I Love Paris • La Marseillaise • Let It Be Me (Je T'appartiens) • Under Paris Skies • Watch What Happens • and more.
00311498..............................$10.99

HYMNS FOR ACCORDION
arr. Gary Meisner
24 treasured sacred favorites arranged for accordion, including: Amazing Grace • Beautiful Savior • Come, Thou Fount of Every Blessing • Crown Him with Many Crowns • Holy, Holy, Holy • It Is Well with My Soul • Just a Closer Walk with Thee • A Mighty Fortress Is Our God • Nearer, My God, to Thee • The Old Rugged Cross • Rock of Ages • What a Friend We Have in Jesus • and more.
00277160 ....$9.99

ITALIAN SONGS FOR ACCORDION
arr. Gary Meisner
17 favorite Italian standards arranged for accordion, including: Carnival of Venice • Ciribiribin • Come Back to Sorrento • Funiculi, Funicula • La donna è mobile • La Spagnola • 'O Sole Mio • Santa Lucia • Tarantella • and more.
00311089..............................$12.99

LATIN FAVORITES FOR ACCORDION
arr. Gary Meisner
20 Latin favorites, including: Bésame Mucho (Kiss Me Much) • The Girl from Ipanema • How Insensitive (Insensatez) • Perfidia • Spanish Eyes • So Nice (Summer Samba) • and more.
00310932..............................$14.99

THE FRANK MAROCCO ACCORDION SONGBOOK
This songbook includes arrangements and recordings of 15 standards and original songs from legendary jazz accordionist Frank Marocco, including: All the Things You Are • Autumn Leaves • Beyond the Sea • Moon River • Moonlight in Vermont • Stormy Weather (Keeps Rainin' All the Time) • and more!
00233441 Book/Online Audio..............$19.99

POP STANDARDS FOR ACCORDION
Arrangements of 20 Classic Songs
20 classic pop standards arranged for accordion are included in this collection: Annie's Song • Chances Are • For Once in My Life • Help Me Make It Through the Night • My Cherie Amour • Ramblin' Rose • (Sittin' On) The Dock of the Bay • That's Amore (That's Love) • Unchained Melody • and more.
00254822 ....$14.99

POLKA FAVORITES
arr. Kenny Kotwitz
An exciting new collection of 16 songs, including: Beer Barrel Polka • Liechtensteiner Polka • My Melody of Love • Paloma Blanca • Pennsylvania Polka • Too Fat Polka • and more.
00311573..............................$12.99

STAR WARS FOR ACCORDION
A dozen songs from the Star Wars franchise: The Imperial March (Darth Vader's Theme) • Luke and Leia • March of the Resistance • Princess Leia's Theme • Rey's Theme • Star Wars (Main Theme) • and more.
00157380 ....$14.99

TANGOS FOR ACCORDION
arr. Gary Meisner
Every accordionist needs to know some tangos! Here are 15 favorites: Amapola (Pretty Little Poppy) • Aquellos Ojos Verdes (Green Eyes) • Hernando's Hideaway • Jalousie (Jealousy) • Kiss of Fire • La Cumparsita (The Masked One) • Quizás, Quizás, Quizás (Perhaps, Perhaps, Perhaps) • The Rain in Spain • Tango of Roses • Whatever Lola Wants (Lola Gets) • and more!
00122252 ....$12.99

3-CHORD SONGS FOR ACCORDION
arr. Gary Meisner
Here are nearly 30 songs that are easy to play but still sound great! Includes: Amazing Grace • Can Can • Danny Boy • For He's a Jolly Good Fellow • He's Got the Whole World in His Hands • Just a Closer Walk with Thee • La Paloma Blanca (The White Dove) • My Country, 'Tis of Thee • Ode to Joy • Oh! Susanna • Yankee Doodle • The Yellow Rose of Texas • and more.
00312104 ....$12.99

LAWRENCE WELK'S POLKA FOLIO
More than 50 famous polkas, schottisches and waltzes arranged for piano and accordion, including: Blue Eyes • Budweiser Polka • Clarinet Polka • Cuckoo Polka • The Dove Polka • Draw One Polka • Gypsy Polka • Helena Polka • International Waltzes • Let's Have Another One • Schnitzelbank • Shuffle Schottische • Squeeze Box Polka • Waldteuful Waltzes • and more.
00123218..............................$14.99

HAL•LEONARD®
Visit Hal Leonard Online at
www.halleonard.com